COPPERHEADS

AMAZING SNAKES

Ted O'Hare

Rourke

Publishing LLC
Vero Beach, Florida 32964

www.rourkepublishing.com

PHOTO CREDITS: Cover, title page, pp. 4, 8, 10, 14, 17, 18, 21. 22 © Lynn M. Stone; pp. 10, 12 © George Van Horn; p. 17 © E. R. Degginer/Bruce Coleman, Inc.

Title Page: *A southern copperhead tests the air with its darting tongue.*

Editor: Frank Sloan

Cover and interior design by Nicola Stratford

Library of Congress Cataloging-in-Publication Data

O'Hare, Ted, 1961-
 Copperheads / Ted O'Hare.
   p. cm. -- (Amazing snakes)
 Includes bibliographical references and index.
 ISBN 1-59515-145-1 (hardcover)
 1. Copperhead--Juvenile literature. I. Title. II. Series: O'Hare, Ted 1961-
Amazing snakes.
 QL666.O69O39 2004
 597.96'38--dc22
                          2004008016

Printed in the USA

CG/CG

table of contents

copperheads

Copperheads are members of the *Crotalidae* family. Like all snakes, copperheads are **reptiles**. The copperhead is a **venomous** snake. It gets its name from the color of its head, which is like the color of a new copper penny.

The venomous cottonmouth, or water moccasin, is the copperhead's closest cousin.

Much of the copperhead's head and body are the color of copper.

where they live

Copperheads live in the eastern United States and in Texas. They live mostly in dry leaves, rotten logs, stone walls, wooded hills, and piles of trash. There are usually ponds, streams, and swamps nearby.

The copperhead **hibernates** in dens during the short, cold winter days. As the days grow longer, the copperhead likes to lie in the sun's warmth.

The northern copperhead lives in the eastern and central United States.

This broad-banded copperhead lies in leaf litter.

Did you Know?

Copperheads are usually about 3 feet (1 meter) long.

what they Look Like

The copperhead's thick body is covered with scales. Each scale has a small ridge down the middle. Its light brown body with dark markings is easily hidden in piles of dead leaves. This makes it well **camouflaged**.

The Trans-Pecos copperhead lives only in western Texas and parts of nearby Mexico.

Hidden by its coloring, an Osage copperhead coils on dry leaves.

their senses

Copperheads stick out their tongues to pick up the scent of their **prey**. The **Jacobson's organ** in the roof of the snake's mouth analyzes the scent. In this way the snake learns what is nearby.

The eyes and the two **heat receptor pits** on the snake's face tell the snake about the location and size of the prey. The copperhead strikes as soon as the prey is close enough.

The copperhead uses its long, forked tongue to sense its surroundings.

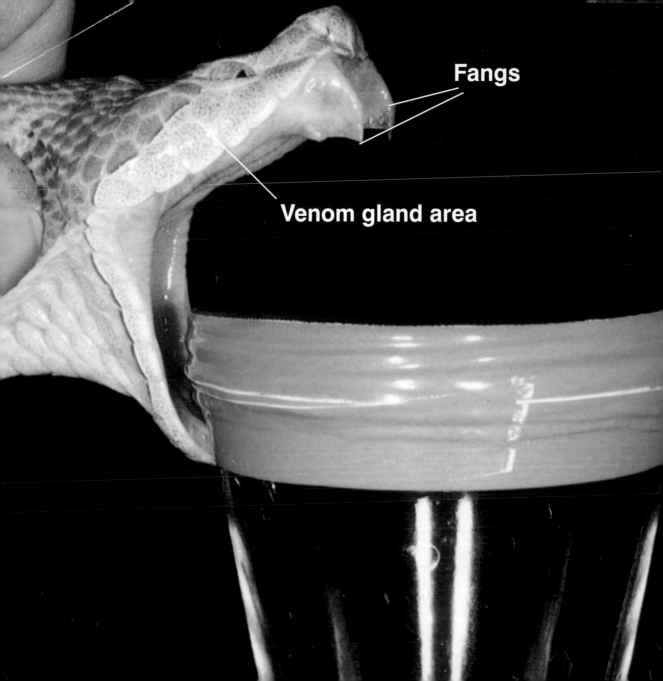

Fangs

Venom gland area

the Head and Mouth

The copperhead has long, hollow fangs. These are folded against the roof of the mouth. The fangs are extended when the snake bites prey. Muscles around the **venom** glands shoot the venom through the fangs and into the prey.

A venom collector opens a copperhead's mouth to force venom from the snake into the glass jar.

The snake's jaws stretch. This means the snake can swallow the animal whole. The windpipe goes from the throat to the front of the mouth. This lets the snake breathe while it is swallowing prey.

A copperhead stretches its jaws to swallow a mouse.

Baby copperheads

The copperhead mother has between 1 and 14 babies in the late summer or early fall. The baby is about 8 inches (20 centimeters) long and has a yellow tail. The young copperhead will shed its skin about 10 days after it is born.

A mother copperhead gives birth to live young, which will soon leave her and crawl off on their own.

Did you Know?
Birds, pigs, and other snakes eat copperheads.

their prey

Mice, lizards, frogs, insects, and birds are prey for the copperhead. Young copperheads wiggle their tails to attract prey. While the prey watches the tail, the snake bites the animal. The copperhead swallows its prey head first.

The great-horned owl is one of the birds that eats copperheads, although it risks death from the snake's venomous bite.

A copperhead finds mouse prey by sensing the heat of its body.

their Defense

Copperheads lie very still when an enemy approaches. They lie camouflaged in dead leaves. Copperheads do not like to fight.

If a copperhead is disturbed, it **vibrates** its tail back and forth. If the enemy comes too close, the copperhead strikes.

Copperheads lie quietly unless they are disturbed.

copperheads and People

Copperhead venom does not often kill people. However, it can make the person sick and damage the tissue around the bite.

Scientists are studying copperhead venom. It may be very valuable in finding out more about human blood.

A southern copperhead pulls back its head to begin eating.

Glossary

camouflaged (KAM uh flazhd) — disguised by fitting in with the creature's background

heat receptor pits (HEET ree CEP tur PITZ) — parts of a snake's face, which give the snake information about the size and location of its prey

hibernates (HIGH bur NAYTZ) — sleeping or inactive, usually during the winter

Jacobson's organ (JAYK ub sunz ORG un) — the part of a snake that analyzes a scent the snake has picked up

prey (PRAY) — an animal hunted and killed by another animal for food

reptiles (REP TYLZ) — animals with cold blood, a backbone, and scales or plates

venom (VEN um) — poisonous matter that some snakes use to injure or kill prey

venomous (VEN uh muss) — containing poisonous matter

vibrates (VY BRAYTZ) — moves back and forth

index

Further Reading

Feldman, Heather. *Copperheads*. PowerKids, 2004.
Richardson, Adele D. *Pit Vipers*. Capstone, 2004.
Wechsler, Doug. *Pit Vipers*. PowerKids, 2001.

Websites to Visit

www.enchantedlearning.com/subjects/reptiles/snakes/printouts.shtml
www.42explore.com/snake2.htm
www.wf.net/~snake/copperhe.htm

About the Author

Ted O'Hare is an author and editor of children's nonfiction books. He divides his time between New York City and a home upstate.